REVOLUTIONARY EROTICA

Poetry by

Nathan Jones

SAJETANIRA PUBLISHING GROUP

P.O. Box 211-0211
Oakland, CA 94604 USA
www.sajetanirapublishing.com

Copyright © 2003, 2010 by Nathan Jones

Editors: Lisa A. Zure and Charlotte Y. Williams

Cover Photography © 2003 Faiza Ali - www.faizaphoto.com
Cover Design: Faiza Ali
Art Directors: Faiza Ali and Nathan Jones
Cover Concept: Faiza Ali and Nathan Jones

Library of Congress Cataloging-in-Publication Data
Jones, Nathan
Revolutionary Erotica & Other Poems/Nathan Jones
ISBN: 978-0-9800747-6-5 (pbk. : alk. paper)

Dedicated to my family and friends and to those who have had patience, love, and faith in my dream. This book is the result of many inspirational prayers, long days and nights of manifesting the gifts of our Creator. I am believing that whatsoever I set my mind to it can be achieved and accomplished. Always believe that the Creator and our ancestors are guiding us with their positive energies.

for Geraldine M. Gray

love has no definition when I think of the blessings you have given me

words cannot express or convey the joy and peace you bring to me

comfort is knowing your saintly prayers are always in my corner

the tenderness of the spiritual food you feed me nourishes my inner-person

grace and elegance are synonymous with your wisdom and knowledge

your dreams for your children are come true,

I thank you for the love, mama.

Acknowledgments...

The first thanks goes up to the Creator from whom all blessings flow. I want to thank my Mama and Daddy, and all of my family members who believed in my process. The families and communities who have shown their love and support in countless and endless ways. The elders and ancestors who have kept me on the right pathway. Thanks to my brothers & sisters (Nolan, Money, Gee-Gee, and Kenny). Love goes out to all my friends who go back to Bella Vista, McChesney, Oakland High, College, and all the many places far and in between. You are not forgotten. And to my inner sanctum, Angel, Willie, Eric, Paul, Andre, and Elgin. Thank you brothers for being my inspiration, my rock, and my support throughout all the uncertain times. For those who go unmentioned, you know who you are. Luxor & New Village, you laid the foundation for this project. Seyana Mawusi. Another Taurus has done it! Blessings and Peace be unto all who take this journey with me. Without you, I would not be here. JBG thanks for Asjua. Dennis and Faiza, you are the icing on the cake.

Love and respect,

Asanta Sana

Contents

Chapter I – Reflections

Chapter II – Love

Chapter III – Soul Searching

Chapter IV – Alienation

Chapter V – Openness

Chapter VI – Evolution

Chapter I

Reflections

African in America

Being an African in America
one cannot help but feel
his dual identity.

His dichotomous nature is
what sustains his very presence
existence and essence in a land
that recognizes him not.

An Afrikan Speaks of Home...

You are an abyss in my heart, Afrika

My face is full of your blood

These hands God gave me work to come home

I, an Afrikan speaks of the rivers in the Congo

I daydream of the warm summer nights, under

Your heaven

I once sat on a throne, drinking the finest nectars

My kingdom was a dominion of prosperity,

My children played freely in our Garden of Eden

Oh! Afrika, how I long to kiss the soil of your beauty

This continent many called "dark" holds the keys to the
Universe

To life, civilization, and many lands of forgotten nations.

Afrika, my face is full of your blood,

Oh, how I long to return home

To the shores of your warmth and beauty

Afrika, I cannot forget you.

Language Change

Language change

Linguistic strains

Mental chains

Communication tamed

Re-defined over time

New verbiage

Our tongues entwine

Like southern vines

Around Germanic

Romantic discourse

Enslavement has forced

Inventive dialects

Neither Mother's nor Father's tongue

Shades and shadows

Memories lost

Yet we understand in codes

Created by a will to survive

Pains from separation's trauma

Rites of passages

Lives taken during the *Middle Passage*

Voices of European savages

Pigeon tongues, tongues shackled

Dual identities form   *dichotomies*

Human survival is the norm

Dichotomies circumvent,

We constantly invent

Ways to communicate,

Djembe, *Bata* to *Banjo*

Bamboulas to banzas

Tambourines to gourds

Marimba to pan flutes

Beat to feet, *Nicolas* to *Savion*

Slap, Tap, to Rap

Stomp to Step, Step to Stomp

Handbone to Jazz tones

Lady Day to *Nina Simone*

Language change

Blues to Blue Notes

Codes of the past

Now we laugh to mask the pain

Funny, Funny, Funny-*Blackface*

Our DNA always finds a way

Many think it's about the *"Cool Pose"*

Now we communicate in European *"Prose"*

Verbal poets emerge and unfold

Pioneer...

walking through uncertain shadows of death
tattered clothes hang from decrepit half-cadaverous bodies
zombie states of minds searching through canopied jungles

survivin' on passages passed down from sagacious griots
telling on North Star woven in elaborate blanket patterns
tilling in the Sun, hoping for Moses (Tubman) to come

muddy waters
   leeches
     snakes
  parasites
    gators lurk

while blood-hounds lose scents and trails
panting after flogged, whipped, tired souls
       pioneers
        pressing
         anxiety

on Freedom's roads, Maroon passages

Quilombo's and Palmare's trails forged by Spirit-Life

African ancestral Gods on "high" alive

(Shango, Obatala, Ogun, yes! Yemaya)

in sight, Sankofa rites

Mighty Clouds of Joy--liberation calls!!!

Toussaint Citadel sits high in God's paradise

watchful eyes hiding behind isolated façade

w

    a

      i

        t

      i

        n

          g

a day's journey turns to a week of suffrage

10,000 strong. Rebellion! Insurrection! Uprising!

blackness meshes into darkness and light becomes blackness

liberation had her songs of "freedom"
while Bob was only a distant echo in the wind
whistling and whispering in marsh lands
                        singing for Jah's people
                                blood-filled eyes
terrified, dying for life, dying to live
underwater caves, lush wastelands, and shanties   solaces
hiding grounds for rebellious blanches-femmes pirates
pushing up against phallic noir points
in guise to act as quasi-Messiah for
                        disillusioned
                                stagnated
black bodies, but Rasta is Irie -like- I-and-I philosophy
Haile Salassie-I (Rastafarian
-ism) -separations schism
likes his femme creamy like the inside
                        of his chew-stick
pioneerin' too many roads to Freedom!

Out From the Dark We Ascend

Out from the dark we ascend like a lotus plant

we travel throughout history like a joule, a unit of energy

a force like *Newton's* neutrons moving through a distance of one

meter in the direction of that force,

We explode in history like an *Atomic* bomb

dispelling the myth of uneducated Africans whose

intellect rivals the talents of *Einstein*, yet surpassing his

In the 21st century we are the hope, the pride, and the dream

of the formally enslaved Africans, 145 years removed from chattel slavery

and I represent the 5th generation of freedom, a descendant of a strong willed

african from the shore of the *Canary Islands*, who escaped the jaws of slavery *two*

years before the *Emancipation Proclamation*

From the degradation of the *Godchaux/Jonas Sugar Plantation* to *Bertrainville* to *New Orleans,* to the blessed

Hypolite, Papa, Nolen, Roland, now me

the blood of freedom flows through my veins, constantly

we reinvent ourselves like the *Phoenix,* altering our invisible existence

a ritual is met...

my silent rage is serenaded by controversial hip-hop anthems like

Fight The Power (PE) and *Fuck the Police (NWA)*

syncopated with rhythmic bass shootin' my subconcious

leaving holes bustin' at the seams...screams! screams!

i watch my 3rd eye vision fade

blood cascade over hazy stained unstable foundations

while verse and prose are the only wars I win hands down

i shadow box with Newton's law of gravity staying afloat

running! dodging! hiding! and bouncing between checks - check it!

I'm emasculated and castrated by *Amerikkka's* white picket fences

in my night and day mares

potatoes and rice sashay across my mind

my daughter comprehends my ends with-"ok daddy!"

my ritual is met with pit-stops to *Mickey Ds* and *B King* (unhealthy sting operations)

savoring the morsel of a processed chicken meal and fries

we step over the homeless, signs in hand "I'll work for food."

coins drop in a paper cups, watching hopeless dreams being fulfilled, momentarily

Prayer House Apostolic Church throws out a raft for salvation

but my *Mothership* was floating upon eclectic trips

righteous words and scripture couldn't save me

nor harmonious chants and voices laced with spiritual strings or bass

that curdle my blood stream

i embrace my daughter for dear life

praying that a Marvel character would liberate her

from the *Deluge* of life's pressures

i close my eyes tight and wish upon *North Star*

because many a lotus grew

and originated

from the black of my mind

Brothas Be...

brothas be battling Babylon while

bomb shelling poison to da babies,

maybe they helped create lives at stake,

pushing and peddling drugs,

cuz thug is the mentality,

living pseudo-life styles, a dead man's reality

pimping a surrealistic paganistic devilish trip,

just to sip the "Amerikkkan Dream"

love Amerikkkan style enough to drive a "brotha" wild.

dead and gone like a stillborn child.

mama didn't raise murderers, pushers, and pimps to

span a generation of empty vessels,

hollow like a *Columbus* voyage.

dead Souls spreading death to young chocolate souls,

hot like coal, fuckin' up many positive would-be molds

silly ass simps, don't know that slavery is mental,

like an imp that pimps you to take negative actions on

your own Black seeds, not knowing

you choppin' down lives like acres of weed

sold and smoked, as you choke, taking a toke to make

your scrill screwing, the pill, she chills,

a baby born, and Babylon exalts the ills.

Tuskegee, Aids, Ebola...

brothas don't be knowin'

conspiracy is white supremacy.

I mean the point is to change the joint.

the joint of fast cars, fast women,

fast cash, fast ass, and fast lives

that don't make the night or dawn because

a mentality and respect for life is gone.

but brothas be knowin'

that the caged bird sings, behind bars, helping to create

more laws while the freed is scarred, soft and not hard, but pressed.

oppressed, depressed, suppressed, and hard-pressed to escape

babylon's chores

brotha's need to be knowin' that the end is near.

slavery is mental and there's much to fear.

It's past time, we need to change our minds

can't afford strange fruit

dangling from the vines of

estranged Black Thought. The price is too high

for Black Souls sold and bought.

How can heaven forgive us

If we slit our own throats?

If deadly conspiracies

dictate our reality

the inevitability is   our people's fatality.

Distant Beat

I am not a simile, metaphor, or a fading symbol.

This you hear is not a breeze softly blowing a tree.

I am not a black strip of asphalt being trampled over.

It is I who express emotions of laughter, pain, and joy.

I cry rivers because I exist, here on Earth,

My voice sings like a choir moving a congregation,

These are the designs of my humanity, my voice.

I speak them, and my hands write them.

I am a poet.

Is it my soul you hear drumming against your heart?

Or am I just a phantom lurking in the dark?

I am not a fading symbol, simile, or metaphor.

this emotion called love...

What is this strange and yet sometimes painful emotion known as love? Why is this one emotion so powerful, it causes the most rational of minds to succumb to its precarious nature? Love is as a legion of a million eclectic spirits who roam from person-to-person, aimlessly setting stoical hearts ablaze with passion; drudging through high plains stalking unwanted and unfathomable prey. But what is this emotion called love?

God only knows that this wretched emotion lies undetected like the nature of a gator, floating silently in a green murky swamp, patiently awaiting its prey, unsuspectingly attacking. But what is this emotion called love? I cannot apprehend, let alone comprehend, this uncanny snaky-like entity that burns through the bone and marrow of pure, unadulterated, and untainted straight-and-narrow souls.

This emotion is so dangerous, it causes men avarice and jealousy, women to possession, children to laugh and smile, mothers to cry, and fathers to die. It sends unfamiliar and unrecognizable chills through-and-through the hollowness of human bodies. What is this emotion called love?

Lethargy would be its best friend if it were not for the sweet and savory love affair it maintains with its bubbly mate passion.

Loneliness would be its home if it were not for the empty vessel it inhabited ephemerally throughout the eons of time. But I of rational and sound mind still have the audacity to question its true intentions, without hesitance and fail

… what is this thing called love?...

I tell you, until this day, and as we embark upon and pass through to another millennium, even Momma and Papa cannot explain to me why this emotion called love continues to have so many different effects on people. I'm only forced to ask the Creator where does He stand in terms of explaining this capricious entity that continues to hackle at my mind.

What is this damned thing called love?

Chapter II

Love

On The Eve of My...

Anticipating your call as I reminisce on your delicate silhouette

Sitting in front of my computer, consumed with your fragrance

Staring at the four corners of my room

Illuminated with deep thoughts

Of you

On the eve of my...

Remembering on your scintillating scent...heavenly

Allowing myself to be entranced, as I mesh with you

Sending ripples of chills down the contour of your

Delightfully

       immaculate

          anatomy...

Wanting to caress she

On the eve of my...

Running my tongue

Along the mystery of your curves

Sweet

    slow

        motion

            …octave rising

Perfumed visions running through my mind

Enchanting

On the eve of my….

The memory of the mystery

In your soulful brown eyes

It's no surprise

Your ebony energy makes my nature rise

On the eve of my...

Fullness is you lying by my side

Your head on my chest while my hands

Massage the softness of your breast

Your back, your waist, thighs, and hips…

Did I miss the fullness of your lips?

And the soft full lashes of your almond-shaped eyes

Brushing my skin like butterflies

Not to my surprise, here I lie

…dreaming… on the eve of my...

     Lost in the sweetness of your

     caramel pleasant

          honey-filled

              Nubian

                   Beehive

All on the eve of my......

Got Me Thinking

I began speaking in archaic Kemetian as the
       warmth of her nature
caressed my face like a Sahara breeze…
       It felt so good
Good like
       listening to *Miles' Sketches in Spain* while
          strolling under Andalusian moonlight
off the coastal shores of Moorish antiquity.

       So, I went to church
and those who know me understand
sanctuaries, like
temples, churches, synagogues, and mosques
are places I rarely visit.
But this woman had me in church
       praying to the Most High, quietly
       I knew this was deep.

Deep enough for me to ask God, "What is up?

Is this my time? Are you going to bless me with a union
like Sheba and Solomon?"

She had me searching the Holy Bible, looking for the scripture,
He who findeth a wife findeth a good thing.

Now you know a brotha was open.
She didn't know that she was Isis, Cleopatra,
Makedah, Nzinga, or any of the Queens
mentioned in my historical cipher.

She was golden sapphire, rubies, diamonds, and black pearls.
And I wore her love like a blood vessel wrapped around
my heart.

Her eyes were deep soul eternal
full of heat and passion like the Earth's crust.
I knew this woman, and she
knew me.

And I was drawn to her like a saint to a revival

realizing my spirit

would be full.

In the Moment...

In that moment I learned to breathe again as

She conjured up that good-good JuJu that I once remembered

My thoughts became translucent like a lagoon

hidden in a remote tropical island tucked away

somewhere in the South Atlantic

In that moment, Love Was Manifested

My mind went soaring across the sky that night like an eagle in flight as I heard her voice whispering wishful euphonies of poetic & prophetic verse coercing and strumming a rhythm song

in my

ear,

in my

mind,

in my

soul,

and

in my spirit. Full I was like a 5-course meal

Reminiscent of how wonderful, sensual, and passionate

it was to share a stolen moment over

a cool glass of guava and mango, as the residue from the

fibers lingered on our lips, and we chanced to consummate with a liquid embrace and chocolate kiss...ooh a chocolate kiss

lips/tongues/spirits all 3 meshed

and we confessed of how blessed it was,

this stolen moment

as we intertwined over an ageless & priceless time,

refined and destined like celestial...

celestial Ethiopian

honey wine...

My spirit remembered that good JuJu it once missed, as she conjured up that tropical bliss

her conversation was peaceful incantations

heavenly sensations, lavish and lush, caressing the contours

of my mentalect, as I checked and respected her energy NOW

our synergy,

fabulous of thought memories not lost

and the sounds, and the sounds: philharmonic, euphoric, mellifluous like a Coltrane/Miles tune

I feel high inside, ooh so high and not the kind of Irie Blue Mountain region high one gets from the H-E-R-B, herb... but a cosmic, ethereal, spiritual Universal high

the kind God gives when you know this woman is, DAMN,

fly, a true blessing in disguise

Satiated by fate's calling as I called her name, and I, and I, and I, YES I call her name

as she leaves indelible impressions on my brain

a holistic spiritual chain locking me in for a win-win

I slightly grin with a mischievous gesture, feeling like Lester Young, the King of Kool

writing her name in ancient Sanskrit, hieroglyphics, and Adinkra symbols

obsessing about our first trip to Abu Simbel

She's got me shimmering with visions of peculiarly exotic places

Traveling in time, in the now, moving to the rhythm of a melodic time signature with her

one-on-one loving from the dusk-to-dawn, titillation/elation/fascination/stimulation/peaceful sensation

We both yawn and yearn for eternal moments of bliss, our love a perfect fit

A

delicate liquefied K-I-S-S, kiss

This Miss, I cannot miss as I perpetuate my discourse

to take a course in her light of being...in the light of her being, and yes I'm seeing

causing me to say

"To be or to be with her is the ultimate question"

As I prepare my lessons, I dissertate in a language of divinity/serenity/equanimity

Confirmation of love, with all its amenities

Savoring my life/my life/my life in her sunshine

Discovering and recovering a lost pyramid of hope

as the walls of distrust and pain slowly dissipate

In that moment I felt that good-good Juju

she conjured up, that made me feel

a connection/reflection

In that moment...

Soul's Confession

She takes my words at face value, not metaphorically

My subtle seductive intent as verbal nonsense, distance

We are just friends? What can I conclude?

What can I infer?

Inside my emotions are like waves crashing up against

Sand shores

Knocking over sand castles, realizing creation is ephemeral

Remembering the teachings of Tibetan Sand Sculptures

Nothing Lasts Forever!

Swimming in darkness to her amplified melodies,

Half-drowning

From her sea of painful interludes, sometimes crass

Soul-searching for solidarity songs, wet from monsoon
Teardrops

My soul confesses with inhibition delicately whispering

I tell her, I have just written an expose of the millennium

Realizing it's a cry to let Her understand I am wet

I am still wet from her sea of words and I tell her I just

Finished bathing and She believes me

We are petrified of the uncertainty of the world and each other

We embrace like family sister/brother remotely islanded

Amidst a tempestuous storm, keeping each other warm

Until the next episode begins

Clouds part and rainbows allude to sunshine colorfully
Iridescent

Looking up not fathoming her sincere warmth

Knowing I'd gladly relinquish my humanity for Her

Shimmering with fear, half-heartedly, I whisper

Save a place in your heart for me

Something inside tells me she will

My hands are her tissue wiping her estranged tears away

We laugh and cry again again and again

I've loved her as a day in God's mind and she

Doesn't understand why

I don't understand why either, but my soul is confessing…

Addict

Savor the moments we share.

Reminisce on the love we've made.

Let not any doubt about my love

Creep into the annals of your mind.

I love you like an addict loves his habit.

Subtle Scent

She left a subtle scent checking for me, discreetly…
A chestnut-colored hue, Ashanti almond-shaped eyes
Clothes hanging loose, hiding her gold and sapphire
Treasures, aloof, laced with a seductive decadence,
Quietly calling my name, but not understanding why?

Inspiration has been a hollow space in a compartment
Hidden away in a remote area in NASA's space shuttle,
Until she reached out with her spiritual umbilical cord
Touching me like a tornado sweeping Elijah away into
Paul's third heaven. Blessing me.

Softly she pushes her wetness against my ballpoint pen
Spreading my ink over the canvas of her earth, creating
Sonnets, quatrains, cinquains, haikus
Phrases, metaphors, poetic verses
Forming passionate tones, highs and lows as she moans

I inhale her chocolate kisses, allowing her

Rainbow-colored love to infiltrate my body

Like an addict injecting heroin

Into his veins. I'm "high" caught in a trance,

Like a zombie

Wandering through a Haitian countryside, looking for my

Next victim (vixen)… a conduit to

Transfer "a disease of love"

She put a spell on me that only God can break…

Aqua Fresh!

Buckets of rain fall from heaven,

Leaving eternal and indelible
Impressions on humanity;

Adam's lost paradise and Noah's vice,
Waters of heaven and hell,

Complementing nature's imperfections.

My flesh encapsulates God's pleasure,

His beauty, and His wrath
Simultaneously causing conjecture to overwhelm

My soul; solace,
Perpetuates a deep unrestful river of ambiguities,

Gray clouds of inquiries.

Earth and I swim in the same cesspool of uncertainty,

Only to find endless unrest. Tell me! When will the rain Cease
to eradicate? Before it turns over souls like

Unstable gravesites in a New Orleans cemetery.

Walking…

Walking around my home suspicious

Looking outside cornered windows

Watching

Crack being sucked up by my family

Vampires sucking the blood from

Unsuspecting innocent victims, bystanders

The dawn sets in

Chants are faintly echoed in wind

Holistic chants and prayers, syncopate in Baptist rhythms

The *Holy Ghost* is trapped in the sanctity of the sanctuary

And God's unchanging hands don't rescue the wretched

God's oasis is right across the black asphalt

Where are the spiritual warriors, while war is waging in the streets?

Voices are loud and faint, creating nightly musical rhythms

Caricatures distorted cacophonies distress my sleep patterns

Prostitutes stroll *Webster* thinking salient strolls go unnoticed

But son (Sun) misses nothing-questions ensue?

Playing in the backyard lost in his world of plastic action figures

Innocent and not affected by the world outside of his world

He's protected by high canopy fences and bushes

Camouflaging his peaceful oasis

Strangely, unfamiliar, bodies of pale content hibernate in

Old money owned structures

The man's neo-hipster children have returned back to the block,

Babylon, now, a haven for his prodigal sons and daughters of yester-year

Gentrification smells the streets…a twisted odor of unwanted pre-destiny

Evergreen Church is greener with new *Jericho Walls* built to God's

Third Heaven

Suspiciously walking in my room,

Looking outside cornered windows,

Expecting change in paradise

But change is gentrified housing

Laid back living for those who have come back to reclaim

A land deemed undesirable.

Black Pride

Whatever happened to Black Pride?

Did you go on vacation? Have you gone to hide?

Or did you just die?

Do you remember when Black pride was so high,

So high like those circular crazy hairstyles

That drove people wild

Upon sight of African might.

Remember when brothers and sisters were poets,

You know the Black Poets

Or was it the Last Poets;

The words that trickled off their lips were

As smooth as a cool bottle of Moet.

Black pride have you gone to hide?

Remember Angelou-- "Phenomenal Woman" or

"Still I Rise..."

Was that not the epitome of Black Pride?

What about the pulsating words of Brown—

"I'm Black and I'm Proud!" Dare we not say it LOUD!

Black pride have you gotten lost in a crowd,

Where your radiant hue cannot howl?

Remember when brothers and sisters were getting "high" on knowledge and getting strung out on "love"?

Remember when black was beautiful?

Remember when brothers packed knowledge

And not gats?

Remember when Black love was as pure

As a raven from the heavens above!

Remember when musicians were musicians and

Not studio artists?

Remember when EWF--(The Elements) sung about "Devotion"?

Remember when the nigga died and

Black folks were let in?

Remember when the nigga died and

Black folks were let in?

Black Pride, I thought I caught wind of you the other day.

Black pride I thought I saw your face on T.V.

I thought I heard your voice on the radio.

Black Pride do you remember Stokely, Newton, and

Rap Brown?

How resilient, how resonating were the sounds.

Black Pride, did you give up your pride

For a suit and a tie?

Chapter III
Soul Searching

Compromise Not...

Compromise not oneself for others, love and understand

Who you are. And let the pureness of your essence exemplify

The inner-you.

I'm Still Here

Can survival in this onyx shell sustain

all the bloodshed, fears, and tears?

As I recollect on living I think of all the names and pejoratives used to describe me...

Uh let me see. I've been called: "dumb," "destructive," "dangerous," "deviant," "deprived," and "disturbed."

Oh, but it gets better. He's a "drop-out," "delinquent," "dope-addict," "street-smart dude," a "welfare pimp," and "dysfunctional." But I say I am still here.

Yes Lord, I am still here.

Even laws have been passed to isolate me from the mainstream of society as I know it.

I've been Jim Crowed, Grandfather Claused,

written down as 3/5 a person, and now

Three Strikes and I'm Out.

What more can happen to me

before I cease to exist in this damned Nation?

Alas Babylon, I'm still here.

Yes indeed, I'm still here.

Looks like I've failed every attempt to live a life of

fruitful prosperity. If it were not for frustration, humiliation, and anger I think life wouldn't be worth

living at all. But I'm still here.

Yet I'm perceived as impulsive, aggressive,

animal-like, and child-like without fail...having

natural rhythm, sensuality,

and uninhibited expressiveness.

Never is my person seen as poetic, creative,

innovative, avant-garde, and assertive.

But by God! I'm still here.

Yes, I'm still here.

The funniest thing about a lifestyle such as mine is that

I continue to run into brick walls. Think about it,

I'm the last one hired and the first one fired.

I've been "black-mailed," "black-listed," and "blackballed."

And I ask for what? Shoot! If I had a choice I think I'd rather be rejected, prejudged, and discriminated against. But since I don't have a choice in the matter,

I'd better thank Jesus for all His blessings.

Right! Looka here.

I'm still around in this chocolate-covered skin.

Yes I'm still here.

If it wasn't for Grace and Mercy, I'd probably be dead.

Let me tell you, I've been spit on, kicked, shot at,

beat, stabbed, hosed, bit by dogs, even been

hand-cuffed, and thrown in jail.

But look at me, I'm still here.

Yes, that's right, I'm still here.

Man I thought my ancestors had it bad,

but when I add it all up, all of it's bad.

I mean my foreparents were chained, beat, enslaved,

had no human rights, and slave codes were invented to keep
them subdued. And the names were even more humiliating
then the ones I've acquired over the years.

I mean they were "coons," "niggers," "bucks," "pickaninnies,"
"mammies,""boys," and "uncles."

I never knew that when one grew old one became

white folks' relatives and kin.

But yes, I tell you, I'm still here.

We are still here.

Fascinating ain't it, as to how I can still exist in this

Black, Bronze, Brown, Chocolate, Pepsi, Coco Butter, Walnut, Chestnut, Cafe-au-Lait, Mocha,

Auburn, Butterscotch, Marron, Orange, Maroonish, Maures, Moorish, Sudanic, Ethiopian, Onyx, Amber, Olive, Mediterranean, Reddish skin, and still survive the harshest reality, a mound of plights as high as Mount Kilimanjaro, all in this lifetime and yet still be here.

But I am here and I ain't going nowhere.

When I Saw Her

she took me

back 8,000 years

to The Dawn of Eden

a most memorable meeting

desire & expectation

    dreams imagination

    Joy & repetition

when I saw her

when I saw her

Deep Soulful Eyes

You are lifetimes manifested, 6000 years of mother wit.

Your eyes are Heaven's constellations illuminating,

Deep soulful eyes, piercing my existence.

You are Nandi's, Sheba's, and Nzinga's lamentations

Reigning and raining on earth's embryonic creation.

I am a micro-cosmic reflection of your essence, your blessings.

Fill my soul with heaven's arc of love eternal.

Deep soulful eyes, open to me so I can come inside

Your sanctuary and lie in the lap of your

wisdom and knowledge.

Deep soulful eyes, speak to me in your language of divinity.

Tune me in, tune me in, and never let me go, until

Our Creator journeys back for His second coming.

Deep soulful eyes, be my high and my pride.

Eyes soulful and vast, bless me, bless me; cover me,

Release me back to myself like Sankofa returning me

To the sanctity and solidarity of my mother's womb.

Soulful eyes, you are lifetimes manifested.

Edge Of Heaven

I jumped off the Edge of Heaven, peeling back the sky like
Ripened fruit

Relinquishing immortality for a solstice in nature's paradise;
for You.

It was your Ambrosia Earthly aura that compelled me to forfeit
My angelic wings

To dance for a season in the lap of your exuberant ebullience.

Blessing my sight, my insight, while manifesting a divine vision
Of paragonic excellence.

Comprehending not why your bronze essence pulled me from
The iridescent architecture of my heavenly home.

Still not understanding why I leapt from celestial foundations
in Marvel at Earth's creation,

Like Nicolas Cage in the City of Angels; unlike

Cage, my travel to mortality wasn't painful like

An Eastern Monsoon crashing to Earth's crust

Afflicting my angelic being with Humanity's pains.

I jumped off the Edge of Heaven into feminine *Shangri-La*

And in my *Lost Paradise*, I realized I

Left one Heaven, and entered another.

I wanted to breathe Earth's breath,

And all the air I could stand to inhale, ingest, and digest from Her,

For her love.

She had me and not even the universe's treasures or pleasures
Could divert my desire from wanting and needing to

Dive and delve into

Her essence.

I wanted Ebony sensation, and I couldn't care less about

The cost or the *Price of Ticket* for this Destination,

I had to journey to fulfill my eternal Love's occupation.

So I added our love up by 1+1 equaling 2 and dividing by 1
Giving me a perfect number 1.

Realizing that Heaven plus Earth is a divine combination

Resulting in perfection

The Sum of one in unison.

I was Father Sky deeply wanting to make love to Mother Earth,

Needing to find that perfect

Symmetry as represented in the number 8

Which is manifested in the Dogon numeric system.

I jumped off the Edge of Heaven to be in her nature's cipher

And to travel the black sand beaches of Her Earth's canvas,

Because her spiritual physicality coerced and flirted with my

Angelic wings.

And I longed for her like *Jacob for Rachel.*

Our destiny was preordained by the

Great Spirit Himself.

My love rained down from the Edge of Heaven

Superfluously cultivating and blessing her

Sepia, bronze, amber, delight.

She was the cowrie shells by which my foundation of passion
Was laid.

Her voice spoke to me, and my soul listened.

I realized I was no longer viewing from the Edge of Heaven.

I manifested my invisibility and she felt my

Divine spiritual physicality…

All because I took a leap of faith.

Angelic Wings

I remember the Silver and Black

The first night in your hallway

The first touch of your hands

Your eyes

Magic like the Morning Star

A soul finding home for the first time

You asked Jah for a sign

A Raiders' loss with zero on the time

A phone turned off, but a line

Made available for my call

We stood nervous and tall

Love was your angelic wings. Spreading

Reaching out to my heart

I fell in green pastures

Love was no fairytale

It was real, like a resurrecting Christ

Ascending the stars

My heart needed love

Seeking for you and not knowing who?

There you stood reaching out

With your angelic wings, wrapping your

Love feathers around my heart

My cup is full with milk and honey

I wish chance will show her face

Again.

The First Time We...

You were silent, fragile, removed.... beautiful
A vision of loveliness, the past, the present...now the future,
Sweet you were... Sweet...My heart cried
The First Time We...

Smiles, touches, slow movement, a memory unforgotten
19 days, the second month of Spring, I chanced to be with you,
Sweet you were... Sweet...It was the first time we...

Surrealism, fantasy, I thought, reality
... Yes! A silhouetted image
My body remembers...You...My body remembers...You
It was the First Time We...

Chocolate

Chocolate tongues touch

Tongues full and lush

Fantasy melts my imagination

Dripping hot fudge on my fascination

Her body is my

     decadent

         vacation

And I'm giving praise for this erotic sensation

Sticky sweet I'm filled with joy

Knowing I'm her chocolate

Play toy.

Spoiled.

You Know, You Know!

You know you know why your river never runs dry. Woman,
Your love is like

Sweet honey nectar dripping from the Black beehive. As I dive
into a vast

river of chocolate, engulfed and surrounded by the many
ripples and rapids of your

chocolate wetness…. Girl, you know you know why!

I'm like the drone trying to reach the Queen's throne…

You know you know why I love you sista.

You know you know why I've traveled so many rivers to

taste your love: the Nile, the Euphrates, the Tigris, the
Mississippi, the Amazon, and the Jordan.

Many rivers of passion that connect and flow through

many valleys of desires, girl, keep on taking my love higher!

You know why your chocolate rivers never run dry.

When I think of all the reasons why I love you,

You know you know why. Eyes cannot see, emotions cannot
fathom, and sometimes I might drift and roam other worlds,
but then I think, You know you know why! It's because my

eyes are fastened, locked, and zeroed in on Your love.

You know you know why your chocolate rivers never run dry.

Mystery of Love

Love is mysterious, not favorable

Yet at times electrifying.

Love is spontaneous when it occurs

Love is as an elusive dream

A dream that appears to be real, yet isn't.

The zenith is high, natural and frightening

Yet mysterious

Love is God in its purest form.

Love is mysterious.

That's just what it is.

Chapter IV
Alienation

Thick Drops

Thick drops of water fall from the sky

Pounding to earth, mercilessly

Each drop a soul spilling over from heaven

When it hits the earth's surface

It makes an impression....

From Murky Waters...

From the murky waters of the Bayou,

To the muddy waters of the Mississippi,

Under the arcane waters of the Chattanooga,

From the shame of the Geechee Lake,

Still

We continue to rise in pride.

Murky waters of the South with African blood in

Its mouth.

Murky waters speak to Our souls,

440 years old, sold and many

Stories untold. Oh yeah! Murky waters

...Cold.

Darkness

I arise from a depth filled slumber, tainted
with
unwarranted mares stifling my ease,
comatose I remain slippin' into a
peculiar darkness. Searching for a tangible
solace…   reaching…
into Black Hole images
amorphous

Shapeless & eccentric like minds of creatures
roaming Earth's pastures
Unseen by my 3rd eye vision
I'm dizzy from academic missions
from…wishin' and fishin'…turnin' pages and
seekin' sages…
my soul burns
explanations I yearn
blood pressure rises and falls
like Bay Area weather

my search

empty

as I lie comatose

slippin' in

Black Hole spaces....amorphous.

A Soul's Citadel

Heaven protects the enlightened spirits of its angels
The sky cradles the colossal weight of the stars
Our Creator watches the souls of his prophets
Space holds the planets of the Universe in perfection.
A soul's citadel encompasses cryptic spaces of darkness.

Mother protects and nurtures her young with tenacity
Encouragement bonds the souls of mother and child
Sacrifice, patience, love and time create a citadel of trust
Unconditional passions for achievement foster love.
It's the Citadel that protects the soul as a forest covers a
Lake from unsuspecting eyes.

Sacred words from the Holy Scriptures save souls from sin
The shepherd provides hope for his sheep, from the wolf
Pastors and Elders speak words of redemption for their
Congregations, a soul's solace, from the force of a Citadel
Religion shapes the minds of nations, implementing a belief
Ideals, permeating thought with an energy of apparition.

It's a soul's citadel.

Ruth

The Creator has taken you to a place
Where we know all dreams and desires
Are made reality, eternal life

In spite of the absence of your mortal
Presence, we know that your vibrant
Spirit and person resound and resonate
In those who are a part of you

What you have created on this Earth
Is apparent in the wonderful offspring
You left behind, not in vain

Your competitive nature still lives on
In the midst of us all persevering and
Forging forth with energy and relentless
Sweetness

Looking Out The Window

I moved from Jack London's paradise to

Kaiser's industrial wasteland. When the blinds come up and

I look through my window, I see Ham's children

Walking the streets of shattered hopes and broken dreams,

Much like Langston's *A Dream Deferred.*

But I understand that my reality is much like the world of

The Matrix--I took the conscious pill.

The universe in which I exist is not lavish nor adorned like a
Hollywood Disney movie.

When the rubber from my tires kisses the asphalt and travels
Down Harbor Way, it tells a uniquely

Different kind of story; something strikingly familiar,

Much like Spike's *A Tale From The Hood.* If

Dreams were Not Deferred, perhaps many of my stories

Would be that of a *Beverly Hills 90210,* and not a modern day
Rosewood or *Black Wallstreet* tale: the kind of tale that ills

Even a comatose spirit.

As much angst as I experience from day-to-day,

I still find myself feeling like

Ellison's *Invisible Man,* yet the paradox, it would seem, is that I attract more attention than

Wright's *Native Son*: Bigger Thomas.

Why in 1999, and I'm not dreaming as I write this...when

I look out the window, I see not a Henry Louis Gates Jr.

Nor a Cornel West *Breaking Bread* about *Race Matters*?

Instead, my eyes only behold recent historical tragedies.

Brothas being shot, prostitutes selling

God's gift to humanity (insanity), a liquor store on every block,

A *Barber Shop*, a church in a 3-block radius of another church
And a funeral home to complement the death that took place
The night before. *Dead Presidents* seem to thrive from the
Lethal misfortunes of many would-be beautiful

Black potentials.

See! My parents don't boast about the good old days of the '60s.
It's not nostalgic like

Yuppies listening to Motown hits like

Glenn Close and William Hurt in *The Big Chill.*

In fact, they don't have time to chill, nor stop to get caught up
in the moment of passivity:

Cause when the action and Movement end,

We lose sight when we look outside that Window.

Mattie Rich's *Inkwell* shed the best light on a possible *Big Chill*,

But when you check the content, the ills from the Dysfunctionality of the Black family brings one chills.

Aberrant forms of acculturation in its purest form

Perpetuates Afrocentric castration.

Where's the holiness in that?..

Some might ask, How does it feel to be in the

"Land of Milk and Honey?"

My response is, 'soullessness.'

As I move from illusion to disillusion, where a bridge separates Me from the wealth of this nation,

I still think of the white kids at the college on top of a hill--Although Affirmative my Actions might be

No one really gives a damn, about

Me.   Outside my window, there is still isolation.

Pushin' A Pen...
And Receiving No Dividends

Feeling tired like Spenser for Hire. A brotha's soul and mind is
Burning like Hell's fire. My body is metamorphosing into an
Amorphous dimension, feeling the pinch of a meager

Pension, contemplation... dissension... perhaps an

Uprising forementioned

As my energies seek retirement from psychological detention,

My pockets frozen deep in a subtle form of

Matriarchal financial suspension.

Where the brothas at? We need male energy

And balance to create a win-win.

Finding hope to save our Black children,

But finding no means to

Employ or implement hope to save the Poor Righteous
Teacher. Yeah, We be teaching, but the hierarchy is sucking
our blood Like leeches. Hope seems dim, working under
modified Servility, being paid slave wages,

Turning academic pages, hoping to create a

New generation of sages...

But where's the love for Generation X as It Ages?

Praises come in multiple forms.

"He's an asset" a colleague annotates.

"He's a blessing to the Academy" one remarks.

Praises are all I get as the shit gets

Thick like the fat lady who sings. But it's not over.

I feel like I entered The 36 Chambers of the Wu Tang,

Not knowing when the illusion will

Manifest into reality. But my reality is a philosophical fallacy,
Breached in an Afrikan-centered principality. Yet I'm

Pushing a "pen" while my talents are being preyed upon like a
Hen in a lion's den.

Constantly preaching to man-childs in a Promised Land, my
Mission is to pull disillusioned

Afrikan children

From a gutter of disparity, but my efforts

Become undermined and neutralized

By pseudo-righteous charities...Still the

Poor Righteous Teacher speaks and

Sees with clarity. Lost in a community attempting to

Rewrite our history, deconstructing and reconstructing the

Misgivings of afflictions, lies stacked like

Mounds of the ancients in Mississippi still chased

By the "ghost" of masta's hounds. But we, me, he, the

Poor Righteous Teacher is asked to "stick around."

My reflection in the mirror appears to be a back-lash from the
Pre-Civil Rights Movement and the Black Movement all
Intertwined into one...

Still looking down the face of the barrel of a gun.

Feelin' like I'm Public Enemy Number One.

In shackles, mental, economic and financial. This profession

Is not glamorous, sheik nor substantial.

I'm running through dark shafts with fetters on my feet.

This shit is so bleak, I'm forced to

Take my message to the streets.

Surviving the struggle is cliché and old,

It's time for me to break the mold.

Sell me a new line of hope, not a line white as dope.

That shit is for the fiends...But you think I'm bein' mean?

I think it's time for you to come clean.

Pushin' A Pen...And Receiving No Dividends.....

Love is Funny Like Valentine

Love is funny like Valentine

A seasonal type affair

Something you can find in a Vacant Lot

Or in the Air

A flower that grows through concrete

Beauty often unnoticed, discrete

Impressed upon the naked eye

It sees you like a Spy, but never dies

Love is Jazz music,

It feels and sounds the same

As when you first made love to it

It remains

You can't forget the first time

You heard Mile's *Sketches in Spain*

Or Coltrane's *Naima* or *Love Supreme*,

Love is that Blue Note in Jazz

Referring to tones derived from West African

Singing

Finding that flexible pitch which

Lies between standard notes

Commonly seen between

The Third and Flatted Third Degree

Love is vintage like a century-aged bottle of wine

Once you've experienced love without words

You'll begin to understand the texture, the affinity

Love is Afro-Caribbean cuisine

When those multi-spices hit

The contours of your pallet

You'll understand what love is

Love is finally being with the one you're with

...and listening to Luther's *A House Is Not A Home*

Hoping that it's not only for a night

Love is funny like Valentine

A seasonal type affair

Something you can find in a Vacant Lot

Or in the Air

...It's out there...

The Club

She sat in the corner,
The other night
And painted a wishful picture

From her abandoned table
She conjured a magical brush
And began stroking the canvas
Of nothingness

She created all night long
Almond shaped eyes
African ancestral blues
A solidarity of liberation dreams

Hour after hour
An uncertain off white
Canvas was transformed, adorned

Transformed into remembered dream

Hues a consciousness of mind

Recreation of her self

In present time

Chocolate Passion

Harlem Sweetie in Sugar Hill is wondrously sweet
But Oakland has its share of chocolate treats. Not to
Take away from Langston's masterpiece, but ole hell
What about Oaktown's Chocolate Passion elites?

Chestnut sheen pulsates the heart's desire
Creating a Mocha flame of blazing fire. Suffice to
Say that Chocolate Passion come in various flavors
Much too much to be savored.

Black Orpheus blooming the World over, causing all
Brothers to pull over. But I still get a thrill even
Without a visit to Sugarhill.

If you think Oaktown's chocolate passions are fake
I suggest you chill at Festival at the Lake. And
Get a taste of flavors of much delight soothing and
Caressing to one's sight.

Chocolate Passion may be not in the taste of Sugarhill,

Yet leaving many thrills and fashions, always keeping

The brothers dashing to Our Chocolate Passions.

Chapter IV

Openness

Woman's Man

Woman can you tell me what type of man, it
Is that you seek? Don't tell me you want it all,
Or that you deserve it all…?

Woman, I bet you want a man who's
Aggressive yet gentle,
Ruff yet soft.
Intelligent yet understanding.
Direct yet tactful.
Powerful yet humble.
Romantic yet honest.
Controlling yet
Willing to grant flexibility and latitude.
Loving yet mildly demanding.
Sensitive yet iron-clad.
Physical yet emotionally
Understanding.
What kind of man is this? I suspect it is a
Woman's man.

It's Over II

A quiet darkness in the hallway of your space

Formless expressions of loneliness and distance

Overshadows us.

A teardrop becomes your vice, as you slap me, as you slap me

With a splash of torrid vagueness. Emptiness festers like a
Cancer, incurable.

It's over. It's over like the night vanishing into twilight.

Now dawn,

My expectations are merely dreams deferred.

Empty nights of unshared space and moments, painful
Interludes of sadness,

Mourning deaths of her.

Hollowness is loss like souls wandering aimlessly in space

On slave ship searching back for solidarity and peace

It's over, and I cannot get it back. I can't get it back

Like my youth.

A strange voice within speaks of bewilderment,

Of unsafe conditions.

It's over, and I cannot get it back. And I cannot help but think
Of what I lacked inside.

But, it's over and now I cannot get it back.

God! It's over

And I miss her.

Love not Lust!

It was love not lust that caught my eyes

You were talking retribution, reparations, and revolution

Contemplation of you was thick like hot lava

Capped on a mountain top

Flowing over slowly, yet powerful with a fiery substance.

I realized I had so much love to give of myself to you

The kind of down home Southern type love that kept your Daddy faithful to your mama

It was love filled with

Passion

Dreams

Pain

Joy

Struggle

Tears

Fears

and

yes, endless, timeless, like a Solomon and Sheba love affair written in Bible verse but understood by a Nubian mind.

My soul was ready to love eternally

Cuz it was love, not lust, that caught my eyes

You were talking retribution, reparations, and revolution

and my soul was fed

and my mind understood

and my spirit said,

this is love

The Black Man's Beauty

Once called a wood-chucker, a monkey, and a savage brute in his homeland, Africa, thousands of miles across the Trans-Atlantic, his color and character are further diminished. He is called a brute, a koon, a natural athlete, a spook, a darkie, a jigaboo, and a nigger. Names given simply to denigrate and inflict internalized hatred of himself. But what of the pure and unadulterated essence, what of the "well" that holds the key to all the world's hues? What of the beauty of the black man?

The masons of the world, the architects, the scientists, the artists, the inventors, the explorers, pedagogues, the mathematicians, and the sages of ancient and modern African wisdom. What of the beauty of a Black man? How can myths and stereotypes be so powerful that they permeate the heart and soul of our "essence"? One cried out, claiming he was invisible to a culture that refused to recognize his presence. One man had a dream that all would be able to unite in racial harmony. One man spoke on the ills society projects on its native sons. One man cried, by any means necessary. One man echoed, up, up yea mighty race, and accomplish what you will.

One man shouted, I'm Black and I'm proud. And another coined the phrase "black is beautiful." But, I ask, what of the beauty of a black man? Shall we really keep hope alive? The beauty of a black man, the strain on this amazing creation is nothing less than remarkable. Many nights he's cried and sang the ebony blues, yet his soul is not defused.

Did you see that bronze paragon soar through the air? Did you see that ebony powerhouse cover that field in 9.5 seconds flat? Did you hear that riff in his vocal cords? Have you read the literature of Langston, Wright, Dunbar, Mosley, McKay, Everette? But what of the beauty of a black man? I read somewhere that a black man was responsible for the first open heart surgery. I read somewhere that a black man was ingenious for the transplant of plasma. I read somewhere that a brother was responsible for the first surgical separation of Siamese twins.

Did you know that the capital of the U.S. was designed by Banneker, a black man? And I have my suspicions about the Cotton Gin and its inventors. Did you know a black man was responsible for the creation of the cell phone, the golf tee, typewriter, elevator, fountain pen and traffic signal?

But what about the beauty of the black man? I heard somewhere that he is wise, spiritual, intelligent, honest, loveable, loyal, a great family man, a husband, a father, a friend, a lover, a confidant, and a sage.

Did you know that much of your music was created by a Count, a Duke, a King, and the Ambassador? Boy how stressful can the beauty of a black man be? His mentality is oppositional, yet he operates under pressure with his "cool pose" displaying his integrity and openness. But what of the beauty of a black man?

I heard my sistas say the black man's beauty lies in his ebony sensuous skin. Some sistas echo the beauty is in his bald head, that shines like a flame in a dark palace. I heard many sistas suggest the beauty lies in his dreadlocks. Can she run her fingers through your dreads? Yes, you can! I saw many sistas quiver and shiver at the bass in the voice of Barry. But what is it about the beauty of a black man? The beauty is dynamic, regal, pleasant and diversified.

Maybe the beauty exists in his strut, his laid back way of talking, or his jazzy and flarish personality? He's definitely got the ownership on "cool" and he's definitely nobody's fool. But what is the beauty of the black man?

The beauty lies in his essence, his culture, his food, his dance, his song, his color, his presence, his speech, his walk, his intellect, and the universe of his being. A spirit that many emulate but can never replicate… The beauty of a black man.

As I Look Into the Universe Of Your Eyes...

Emotion has caressed and cradled the spirit of your essence
Since the dawn of our ancestors. As I look into the universe of
Your eyes I now understand that your soul has traveled many
Galaxies, enlightened many stars, kissed many milky-ways,
Cooled many planets, Mercury and Venus alike, just to lavish,
To quench, to enhance, and to suffice

My soul efficaciously; Asjua.

As I contemplate and reminisce about the "love" that brought
You forth I search the four corners of my mind and ponder the
Mysterious places you must've traveled to reach the shore of
The womb that bears testimony to your "faithful" and
"Immaculate" spirit. As I look into The universe of your eyes; I
envision worlds you've seen,

The seas and oceans you've swam, the shores you've

Caressed with your precious little feet bestowing

Love on earth with the warmth of Ra's rays unconditionally
Rising and setting like the

Sun, Asjua.

As I look into the universe of your eyes, I inherently

understand That I and your mother were chosen from the foundation of This world so you can teach Us whatever lessons we must Learn. Because of you I now intricately understand that 1+1=3, Which you make complete, Asjua. And so, as I look into the universe of your eyes, I understand that you

Have known rivers and continue to know many rivers.

As I walk through the gateway to reach your universe, I thank The Creator for allowing "Our" evocation which brought you Forth to set lives on paths and journeys of many unknown Fulfillments, which we know will bridge many souls and foster Love in spite of our fears and pains. As I look into the

Foundation of your eyes, and as I look into the universe of your World, Asjua. I say to you thank you for life.

AISHA! AISHA! AISHA! AISHA! AISHA! AISHA! AISHA!

Love for Eternity, DADDY...

Chapter VI

Evolution

Revolutionary Erotica

My phallic point spills wetness all over this page

Every drop takes a new direction in pointillism, artistic surrealism

Each drop creates a different sensation,

Touch, taste, smell, sight, sounds ticking the senses

Like honey from my scepter

We are the Tantra of past/present times

Revolution is the way we create love, eternally

Inhibitions rendered freely

Liberation sexing outside the box of normality

Bodies of silhouetted images

Human clay, Earth!

God's first Adam and Eve, spiritually human, not divine

Exiting sheltered warmth from isolation,

Stimulation, galvanization, tantalization

Stepping into cosmic paradise, rolling their carnal dice

Naked, baptized by heaven's tears

I sculpt you with lyrical clay

You manifest, acquiesce, and evanesce

Time becomes ancient recollections

I cannot decipher romantic Sanskrit, but I understand my personal love script

Love's revelations, mysterious taboos, world's unknown, indifference

Straddling the fences between Afro/Euro sensibility

Duality, duplicity, dichotomy, multiplicities

Complicity of complexities, invisible destinies

Patience is patience

And my nature is complex, perplexed, compelling, next, next, next…

Traveling cultural odysseys

Reflection of a soul's rebirth, terse

What is my worth? What is my value? I am a metaphoric Black Stallion

Loving the sexual drug, the high, the bliss-never dismissed

Experimentation, other colored skins, I'm in, questions abound

Objectifications, fallacies twisted, like political jargon

Accepted taboos of aberrant bullshit! (BS)-unwarranted tests, I flex

Black noise screams from my lips of

Sax ways, jazz ways, ways ahead, dazed…Aged!

Turning musical pages, invoking ancestral sages

Hearing verses of divine speech, vintage

Perfect like Christ's spiritual cipher, non-decipherable

Sacrificing one discipline, for prophesy sake, my inner-poise quake

A soul lost to non-spiritual temptation,

One less predestination, sometimes stress in celestial destination

Revolutionary erotica, the erotic is revolutionary

Tales from the catacombs, underground

Surviving on hollow ground

The dead live on throughout the pages of history

I catch spirits in the wind, like Native Dream catchers

While souls excavated

Exploited like Hottentots backside

Euro sexual African treasured prizes

Colored pussies suffer from neo-colonial rape

Forced sterilization and experimental surgery, vilifying!

Xenophobic pirates decimate my pre-existence

Don't be ashamed of the shamed,

For the same shame causes inter-generational pains

Racists' myths perpetuate ignorant energies

Cultivating dilution, convolution, and pollution

Tarnished and tainted, wearing Fanon's mask

Depth of one's essence is lost like "progressive theory"

And politically incorrect rhetoric

I stand at the juxtapositions of life/death/rebirth

Spiritual intimacy confuses my mind

Like verses from Songs of Solomon

Challenging traditions of sacred psychosexual, metaphysical

And spiritual inter-connectedness, apprehension is my life's "raft"

Traditional rituals become caricatures, distortions of my existence

And now my psyche vacillates as a pendulum   between

Afro-Euro synthesis

An American antithesis

A symbiosis, a mirage of life

Levels of capitalistic conditioning and bargaining

Hope is chronic bliss

Life's corruptions, interruptions

An asili suppressed by Euro odysseys

Like a junkie's hopeless vision of reality

Nigods are vanquished

Straddling cultural identity

Caught up in the plight of others

Sex, love, taboos...

Angelic manifestations rescues my soul

I dance because it is my "Messiah", my liberation

Living between erotic fantasies, lost in a prism of carnal and sacred

Desires to integrate other worlds

Acceptance never achieved, an anomaly always perceived

Experimentations become my soundtrack of lived interludes

Black metaphors keep me dancing in the tenses of time

Diverse women from times past, was it love or a fad? Fading...

Memory of memoirs rarely understood, I understand, over-stood

Encryptions intimacies are scripted on the papyrus of my soul's chest

Passion is lost in a silhouette of kaleidoscopes

Multiple African relationships cultural mixing

Amalgamations (new races/faces) miscegenation once [outlawed]

And hope manifest its complexities in profound moments of anxieties

Provocative lessons in Black and White... strife...we fight!

For an education in necro (death)

Mirroring the reflection of consciousness /unconsciousness?

Rebirth, a new renaissance in humanity

Cultural pride is exemplified

Sold   Bought

       Packaged

         Repackaged

            Pressed

   Distributed

      Manufactured

         Marketed

            Advertised

Managed and

      Produced

We buy! We sell! We buy! We sell! …

And live the lie of perpetuated hells

Cultural integrity is questioned?

Identity is manipulated through

Cultural theft is confusing, misusing and distorting our minds

Minds are not sound because race and sex hounds the flesh

It massages the mind like a 1960's psychedelic drug

Jimi understood the trip, Purple Haze, baby

Music, dance and rhythm cures the curse

Music, dance, and rhythm cures the curse

Music, dance, and rhythm cures the curse

Of Babylon yet the beast lives on

The revolution is erotic, erotic, erotic, erotic…

Thrown Away

We vowed a sacred promise of love everlasting

Tossed away like sour milk, my heart's mind vanquished

Myriad of images flutters through my mind like black hole spaces

Silent screams of torn images, spin uncontrollable like tornadoes

Spinning, spinning, and spinning non-stop!

Splashing tears of pain against walls like paint on open canvas

Spattering wet spots of unforgotten memories

Over the innocent span of multi-colored sheets

Spinning faster and faster, the spots become loss streaks

Like lost souls

Blurred in my mind's Eye

My 3rd eye vision lacks clarity

Now

Torn and writhing on the floor

Picturing faces she has slaughtered in worlds, before

Faces of bronze content resembling my own

Will she ever flee my mind?

Will no other rid me of this vixen?

Still the emptiness festers like cancer

All I roll over on soft multi-colored sheets

To fill my air with heaven's perfume

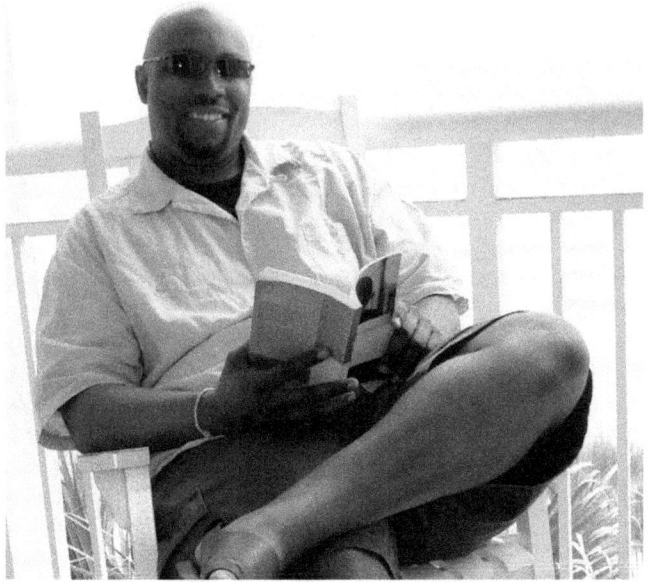

Nathan Jones is a new generation poet, teacher, writer, father and friend whose work is hard hitting, intensely insightful, and alive. With a style deeply rooted in the rich tradition of Black literature and music, this wordsmith stands to make his mark among the admired peers and predecessors. His work is peaceful meditation, a romantic stroll on the Champs Elysees, a delicate tribute to hip hop, and the rhythm and voice of his people.

Other Books by Nathan Jones

Black Man In Europe: The Novel

Black Man In Europe: Micro-Volume I

Excerpts From My Soul: Read Without Prejudice

Forthcoming Projects from Nathan Jones

Letters To My Daughter: How A Dad Became A Father

In The Moment: A Collection Of Poetry

The Paris Chronicles

Love's Reflection

Letters: Voices From The Past

Connect with Nathan Jones Online

www.sajetanira.com